Courage Takes Practice

Written & Illustrated by Amy Scheidegger Ducos

Dedicated to my
brave Olivia,
Don Miller, and Paul Hartley

along with

every kid who needs help
expressing big feelings and
standing up for themselves.

Table of Contents

The Basics of Color Theory

Have you ever noticed that certain colors make you feel certain emotions? This is called color psychology. While reading the book, you will notice the color combinations for each illustrations are meant to highlight the emotions the characters are feeling. *For more color detail, skip to the end of the book!*

 Yellow = Happy

 Green = Hope

 Blue = Sad

 Purple = Creativity

 Red = Angry

 Orange = Alert

Why Learn Color Theory?

Color theory is both the science and art of using color in any kind of visual art form. Artists use color to convey the emotions they want their viewers to feel because as we learned, colors make people feel certain ways. Young artists should learn color theory so that they can better communicate their own feelings in a way others can understand, even subconsciously. This book is made for artists who want to use color to more easily convey the feeling behind their art.

Here are a few examples where you can see the colors and their feelings in action:

New Latina in Town

Chapter One

3

NORTH CAROLINA

ECUADOR

4

Meet Olivia.

Olivia is a nine-year-old artist who just moved

from Ecuador to a small town in the United States with

her family. She has an awesome Mom, who is also an artist,

and Dad, who is a scientist.

She has a puppy named Petey—a pup she can't

live without, mostly because he is Olivia's

enthusiastic and adorable portrait model.

It's the first day of school and Olivia is meeting her fifth grade teachers and classmates. She is excited and nervous, as she always is when school starts. This year, however, Olivia is in a whole new place and has to find new friends.

8

Olivia is pretty green at making new friends and not used to starting all over again.

Her new teachers and classmates half-attempt to pronounce her two last names but they all get it wrong. Olivia pronounces them.... ***Digno Soñador*** (*Dih-neo So-nia-door*).... but no one tries to say it again. "We'll just call you Olivia from Ecuador!"

What is wrong with my names? Olivia wonders. She shrinks down in her seat until school is over.

At home with her parents and pup, Olivia asks if their names are too hard.

"Should we change them? Do people do that?"

"Yes, some people do," says Dad. "But our names are important to us. Digno is your Mom's last name, which means worthy. All people are worthy of love and compassion. And Soñador is my last name, which means dreamer. Which is what you are! You come up with whole new worlds when you paint."

Dad smiles and Olivia rests her head on his arm. "Our names have meaning, you see? Anyone who doesn't try to pronounce them correctly is the one at fault. They are missing an opportunity to learn something about you."

11

"Okay Dad," says Olivia, beaming. "I'm proud of my names."

Mom walks in with a colorful collection of new paint tubes. "Hey, guess what? We got you some new paints to celebrate your first day of school. You have the green light to go give them a whirl, if you want."

"OF COURSE I DO!"

14

Olivia goes to hang her new artwork up in her room. She pins it next to a painting that Mom made for Olivia before she was born, a painting Olivia usually talks to when she is having big feelings.

Talking to the painting, Olivia asks, "Should I go by my teacher's rooms tomorrow and pronounce my name for them?"

There is silence because neither the painting nor Petey could respond, but Olivia decides for herself. "Yes. I will start with Mr. Miller, since he is the art teacher and art is my most favorite, with science coming in second. They are both about pure experimentation!"

The next morning, Olivia goes by Mr. Miller's classroom to tell him the

correct pronunciation of her last names.

"You know," Olivia says, looking down at her feet, "I am an artist.

Or I want to be."

"Thank you for stopping by and teaching me how to say your names,"

says Mr. Miller. "They are not names I have ever heard before but I am

glad you took the time to teach me. I'm sure you will pass the class with

flying colors! I am excited to see your work!"

18

Later that week, Olivia is in art class, drawing a portrait of Petey. Mr. Miller sits down next to her. "Hello Miss Digno Soñador. Who is this furry friend?"

Tickled pink, a huge smile takes over Olivia's face—"Hi Mr. Miller. This is Petey, my dog. He helps me with my artwork."

"Wonderful to have help. He looks like a sweet pup."

"He is. I draw him a lot because he's always moving around. I can get him at all angles."

"Ah, a golden opportunity for quick poses. Maybe you can train him to sit still longer so you can do a detailed portrait painting?"

At home after school, Olivia shows her newest portrait to Petey. He tilts his head, sticks his tongue out, and wags his tail.

"My art teacher likes you, Petey! He said I should train you to sit still longer for more detailed paintings."

HA! Once in a blue moon, Petey thinks, acting like he didn't understand that last part.

Making Friends

Chapter Two

23

A few weeks into the semester, word has started to spread that Olivia

is an artist. Two popular kids in fifth grade, Miles and Madison, are in

Olivia's science class.

"Hi," says Madison, Miles standing beside her. "We like your artwork.

You're good! We have a bake sale coming up and we need posters for

the hallways to promote it. Would you help make us some?"

Olivia is happy to help, especially with something she is good at.

She hopes she will impress her classmates.

26

She gets to work right away! She skips lunch to work on the posters. Her parents even let her stay up an hour past her bedtime to make more.

Two days later, the day of the bake sale, Olivia finds Miles and Madison after last period to hand over her colorfully-doodled posters. They thank Olivia over and over and together they hang the posters along the hallways of the school while all the tasty treats get set up. Olivia's mom even made milhojas—a dessert made of puff pastry layered with pastry cream—to add to all the cookies and brownies other students are selling.

At dinner that evening, Olivia is eating a very traditional Ecuadorian soup called fanesca, a delicious dish made of beans, squash and fish with lots of toppings. It is usually made for Easter celebrations but the Digno Soñadors love it all year-round.

Olivia tells her parents about the bake sale and the new friends she has made. Her parents are happy because this is the most excited they have seen her since school started.

The next day, Olivia is in art class drawing Petey, of course, when she sees Miles and Madison walk by.

She rushes to the door and shouts "Hi!" The pair of them turn around briefly, then look at each other and giggle. They point at Olivia, and then turn back again, whispering to themselves as they walk away.

Confused, Olivia thinks, **What did I do?** She slumps down in her chair, ignoring her drawing. She feels like she is in the dark about something—**but what?**

Feeling blue that night, Olivia is at home with Petey, drawing rain drops on paper. Petey nudges her arm as if to ask **what's wrong?**

"People are mean, you know? Yeah, I guess you do."

Petey had lost an eye before Olivia's parents adopted him. She cuddles Petey on her lap and continues to draw dark storm clouds.

For the last few days, Olivia has no longer been drawing her pup in art class. Today, she's drawing the face of a girl sitting on her own with her head buried in her hands.

Mr. Miller watches Olivia draw with concern.

36

Eating spicy chorizo sausages with chimichurri for dinner, Mom asks

Olivia about her new friends and, out of the blue, Olivia's eyes well up

with tears. Mom and Dad look at each other, not knowing what to do

or say.

They turn the TV to one of Olivia's favorite movies, hoping it will cheer

her up. It works, but only slightly.

The next day, Olivia makes it through her history and English classes without feeling too sad, but in art class, she finds herself drawing images of huge, crying eyes. When the lunch bell rings and everyone packs up to leave, she asks Mr. Miller if she can stay in the art room to eat her sandwich.

"Of course." he says. "But can I ask why?"

"I'd rather not talk about it. At least not today."

He slides a small, flat box across the table. "Here are some new watercolor pencils. Just arrived yesterday." He raises his eyebrows as if to ask, **_Want to test them out?_**

Olivia flashes a mini smile, then starts opening these new pencils.

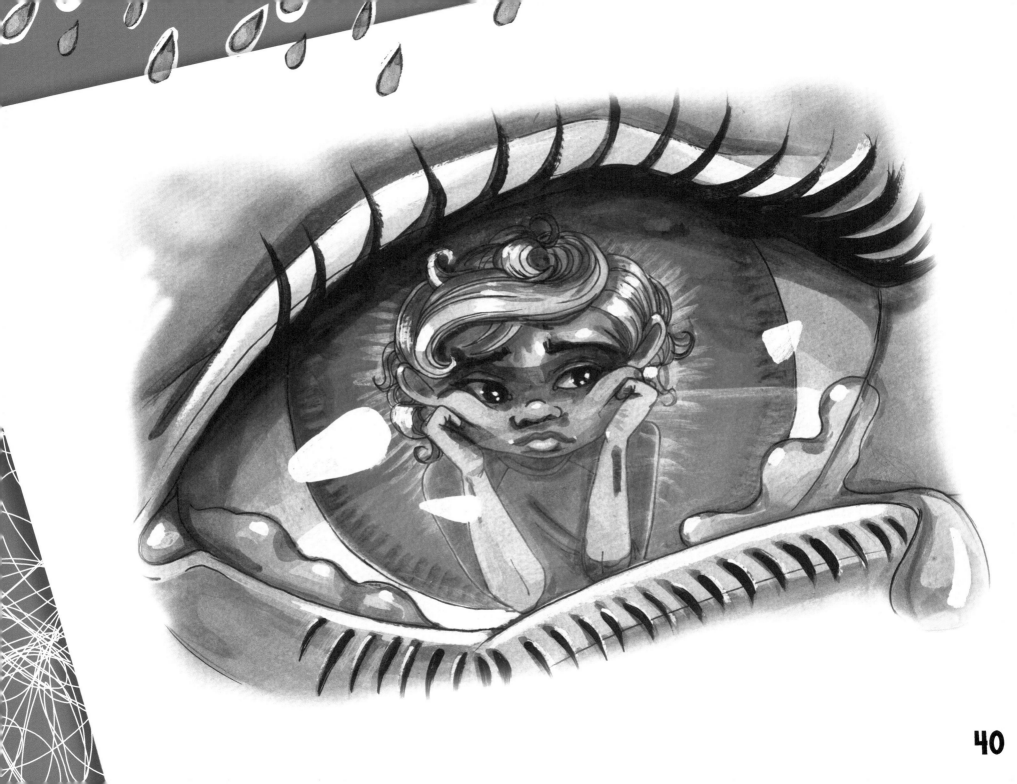

After school Olivia goes straight to her room.

With Petey watching, she faces the painting on the wall that Mom made. "Should I talk to Mr. Miller about Miles and Madison? He might know them and talk to them. It's so embarrassing though, being a total tattle-tale. And what would I even say to him? It's not like I matter much in that school anyway."

Petey rests his head on Olivia and whimpers, seeming to understanding every word.

Keep Trying

Chapter Three

After lunch the next day, Olivia is settling into her seat in science class, when Miles and Madison walk up to her. She's surprised—and happy—and scared. **What do they want?**

Madison flicks her hair over her shoulder, "Hi Olivia," she says. "How are you? Did you hear about the science fair next week? We were hoping you could help us make a few banners for the entrance to the auditorium."

"You'd be doing us a huge favor, " Miles chimes in, shoving his hands in his pockets. "Because no one can draw letters as well as you."

Olivia is so flattered! She agrees to help make the banners. "Of course, anything for science!"

Olivia and several classmates meet in the gym to make banners.

Mr. Miller and a troop of volunteers are also there to help set up

for the fair.

Olivia's heart bursts with relief when Miles and Madison show up

to help her paint.

48

Over the weekend, while shopping with her parents, Olivia asks if she can buy blank sketchbooks for her friends at school.

"Sure," says Mom, excited to hear that Olivia's friendships are growing.

"And could I invite them over for dinner?" Olivia asks.

"Absolutely!" Mom says with a smile.

Olivia spends all night personalizing the sketchbooks with

Miles' and Madison's names. Olivia knows the color yellow

represents joy, so she paints their names in the happiest

yellow she can find.

The next day, Olivia finds Miles and Madison by their lockers and proudly presents their personalized sketchbooks.

"I made these for you both, I hope you like them!"

Thankssss, they both say in a funny way, as if they feel uncomfortable. Their eyes shift back and forth, never landing on Olivia. Then they stare at each other and curl their lips as a clear sign that Olivia was not welcome.

54

Olivia walks away—confused—again. **AGAIN!**

Olivia realizes she forgot to ask Mile and Madison to dinner. *Who knows—maybe a good Latin American meal will make them like me again?* She quickly spins around and walks back to their lockers, and she overhears them talking.

"That **Soñadumbo** girl is too much," chuckles Miles.

"Yeah, like, making some posters at school does NOT make us friends," says Madison, throwing her personalized sketchbook on the floor.

With the thud of the sketchbooks hitting the floor, they spot Olivia.

56

It is obvious that she has heard their mean words. Olivia can feel

her face turning beet red. She feels almost sick to her stomach.

She is . . . totally . . . completely . . . embarrassed!

58

Devastated, Olivia runs to Mr. Miller's art class and hides in the

photography darkroom.

The red safety light is the only thing keeping her from a total blackout.

60

Courage
Takes
Practice

Chapter Four

Mr. Miller comes in, having only seen a flash of color and curls whiz past his office door, and they talk.

Wiping away her tears, Olivia tells Mr. Miller about how Miles and Madison are treating her.

"What you are describing is bullying," says Mr. Miller.

"But they aren't hitting me, or threatening me or anything. I am not sure what they are doing, I just know it hurts."

"Bullying comes in many forms." says Mr. Miller.

"Making anyone feel used, or small, or invisible, is bullying. It seems they have showed their true colors to us both. They could be green with envy because they aren't as creative as you. How do you want to handle it?"

Olivia takes a moment to think. "I can make it through the rest of the day. I will tell my parents tonight."

"Brave Olivia," smiles Mr. Miller.

Olivia comes home after school still feeling sad, so her mom made Olivia's favorite dessert, trés leches cake, in the hopes of cheering her up. But it doesn't help.

Olivia thinks talking about what is going on will make her feel better. So she tells her parents everything.

Dad looks at Olivia with warmth in his eyes. "Our hope is that people appreciate you for that great big heart you have," he says. "Not just for the beautiful banners you can paint, only to be made fun of afterwards. You are an incredible artist, but you're also a whole person. Real friends will want to know all parts of you."

Olivia listens closely as Dad continues. "There is some responsibility on your part, to stand up for yourself if people make you feel bad. Even if Mom and I make you feel bad, we want you to tell us. We are here to listen and learn, too."

70

Mom leans close to hold Olivia's face in her hands. "It takes practice but you can do it. You can do it because you are the smartest, bravest nine-year-old I know. You know that to get better at painting, you have to practice all the time, right? Same goes for most things in life—most definitely standing up for yourself."

"We love you so much, Olivia!" say Mom and Dad, giving her a big bear hug.

"Woof!" says Petey.

It is a sunny but chilly weekend as the leaves on the trees start to turn the colors of Fall. Beautiful dark reds, burnt oranges and golden yellows. A few weeks have gone by and Olivia is feeling better about herself. Miles and Madison have not talked to her since that day she overheard them making fun of her.

Olivia is walking Petey on the waterfront while Mom and Dad pop inside an ice cream shop to get some cones. Olivia stays outside since dogs aren't allowed inside.

Suddenly, Miles and Madison appear, unavoidable by the time

Olivia sees them. **_She turns as white as a ghost._**

"Hi Olivia, is that your dog?" they say in a cheerful unison, as

if they've forgotten she had overheard their last conversation

about her.

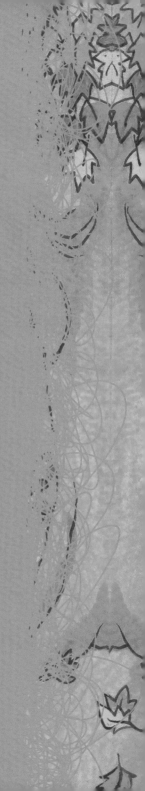

"Erm, yeah, his name is Petey"

"WHOA, HIS FACE IS MESSED UP..."

says Madison...

GASP!
FLASHES OF RED!

OLIVIA HAS HAD ENOUGH! They can giggle and whisper about her when they don't need posters drawn but this is the last straw. White-knuckled, Olivia shouts loud enough for the whole block to hear— . . .

"NO! YOU KNOW WHAT'S MESSED UP—?

Petey went through a lot when he was a puppy but he still loves everyone he meets. What's messed up is how you talk about him—and, and—how you treat people. You only pretend to like people when you need something from them..."

—Olivia takes a long pause. She breathes in and out—

"I'M NOT MAKING ANY MORE ART FOR YOU!"

Miles and Madison roll their eyes and scoff. Madison mutters *"FINE, not worth our time,"* under her breath as they turn and walk away.

Olivia knows that bullies hardly ever apologize, and that's not what she was hoping for anyway. She could tell them how mean they are until she was blue in the face, but she would rather put her energy toward school, art and her family.

Olivia is proud of herself after confronting her first-ever bullies.

But she still feels sad. Petey can sense this and he pulls her down a

creaky, wooden walkway to her favorite spot out on the water where

she can see turtles swimming.

Her parents catch up to them with an ice cream cone filled with her favorite flavor, pistachio (because it's green).

"We heard you stand up for Petey….and yourself," says Mom.

"We're very proud of you," smiles Dad.

"We love you, kiddo," they both beam in unison.

They all hug as the sun sets on the water.

A month has passed and neither Miles nor Madison has said a word to Olivia since that day at the ice cream shop. Olivia is much happier at school now that she had made friends with other kids in her art class, who like painting and drawing as much as she does.

"Thank you, Petey," she says to her furry best friend, "For giving me the courage to stand up to Miles and Madison. Anyone tries to mess with you, they'll have to go through me first. And if anyone tries to mess with me again—well, they can try, but it won't work."

They smile at each other, heads high, full of hope and color, feeling unstoppable.

The End

Meanings of Color Idioms

1. **Being "green" at something** – inexperienced, new, innocent

2. **Having the green light –** to be given permission to do something

3. **Flying colors** – to accomplish something very successfully

4. **Tickled pink** – very happy or amused

5. **Golden opportunity** – a chance to do something that is likely to be very rewarding

6. **Once in a blue moon** – when something happens very rarely

7. **Feeling "in the dark"** – to not know about something that other people know about

8. **Feeling blue** – to feel sad

9. **Out of the blue** – when something happens unexpectedly

10. **Turning beet red** – when your face turns red because you are embarrassed

11. **Total blackout** – a loss of vision, consciousness, or memory

12. **Showing "true colors"** – to reveal one's real nature or character

13. **Green with Envy** – to be very unhappy or jealous because someone has something that you want or you can't do what someone else can do

14. **White as a ghost** – when your face goes extremely pale, usually out of fear

15. **Flashes of Red / Seeing Red** – when someone becomes so angry that it controls them

16. **Until blue in the face** – doing something until exhaustion with zero results

Color Theory Wheel

Blue — the color of sadness & uncertainty

PRIMARY

Indigo — integrity

Purple — the color of spirituality & imagination

SECONDARY

generosity — Magenta

Red — the color of anger & passion

PRIMARY

acceptance — Coral

Orange — the color of energy & action

SECONDARY

Amber — confidence

Yellow — the color of happiness & optimism

PRIMARY

Chartreuse — enthusiastic

Green — the color of hope & health

SECONDARY

Turquoise — balance

Non-Wheel Color Theory

Pink
the color of love
& compassion

is a TINT of red
(red + white)

Gray
the color of
neutrality

is a TINT of black
(black + white)

Brown
the color of
stability &
reliability

is a combination of
2 complementary
colors

White
the color
of purity &
innocence

has no hue at
all because it
REFLECTS all light

Black
the color
of power &
strength

has no hue at
all because it
ABSORBS all light

Printed in the USA
CPSIA information can be obtained
at www.ICGtesting.com
LVHW060720020324

773366LV00005B/44